Historic & Scen Tasmani

MW00906507

Photographs and design by Owen Hughes

Text by Bernice Jurgeit

'GREEN GABLES'

PUBLISHED & DISTRIBUTED BY OWEN HUGHES
17 Elizabeth Street, Launceston, Tasmania 7250, Australia. Telephone: (03) 6331 1481
http://www.computermania.com.au/owenhughes/

First Published 2006
Reprinted 2007

Typeset by Computer Support Tasmania, Lilydale, Tasmania 7268, Australia
Map of Tasmania © Copyright TASMAP
Colour separation, printing & binding: Dai Nippon Printing Co. Printed in Singapore.

National Library of Australia ISBN number: 0-9590145-6-X

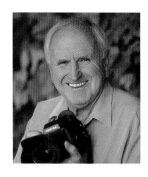

Owen Hughes was born at St. Marys, Tasmania in 1940 and raised on a small East Coast farm where he developed a great love of nature and people. Owen developed a new and innovative style of photography which won him many awards throughout the years including Master of Photography and Fellow of the Australian Institute of Professional Photography. Other awards have included Australian Landscape, Australian Portrait and Australian Wedding Photographer of the Year.

Contents

Front cover: Dove Lake, Cradle Mountain.
Back cover: Penitentiary, Port Arthur.

The moon rises on Great Oyster Bay and Schouten Island, south of Swansea in Freycinet National Park.

Tour boat the Tamar Odyssey under King's Bridge (1864), in Launceston's Cataract Gorge.

INTRODUCTION

Characterised by a gentle lifestyle that has long withstood the rigors of economic, social and political change, Tasmania today retains an eclectic mix of cultural and technological savvy, interspersed with traditional old world charm, across the stretch of an island better known for its diverse physical beauty. This southernmost state of Australia attracts visitors worldwide who come to experience in microcosm a sanctified way of life reminiscent of their forebears. They come also to see first hand what those who live here have loved and protected, the land itself expressed in impenetrable wildness, at times threatening and exciting and beyond the fertile valleys and plains of the interior, the calming spread of beaches and bays.

Tasmania wears her sea borders like a petticoat, the break in land provided by Bass Strait from mainland Australia has served to buffer Tasmania from the rapid coastal developments that have taken hold in the north. It has also assisted in the retention of a simplistic way of life intrinsic to the family dynasties created since white settlement overtook the aboriginal population more than two hundred years ago. The landscape has sculpted the people and their cultural heritage. The first dark skinned people here were synonymous with the land they trod, living and breathing in a synchronised rhythm with the earth. Evidence of Aboriginal tribes suggests this land was theirs for thousands of years before white man came exploring with their civilising culture, foreign, fearsome and fatal. Remnants of these people survived to coexist in modern life, rediscovering their culture and their land. Their past is still etched into the landscape in the form of middens, carvings and caves.

With the arrival of the colonists from England in the early nineteenth century the island changed for ever. They brought with them knowledge and the means to subdue vast tracts of land to sustain the needs of the steady influx of people that was to arrive in the years ahead. The land opened up beneath the hands of their endeavours creating farms for cropping and cultivation and providing space for roads and towns. The soft, fine wool of the Merino sheep continues to grow abundantly on the sheltered pastures of the central and eastern farms while the rusted volcanic soils of the north and west proved profitable for growing vegetables and grazing cattle for milk and beef. The surrounding waters that once knew a thriving whaling and sealing industry today support scallop, fish and oyster farms. Agriculture and aquaculture are the lifeblood of many Tasmanians whose families have known nothing else since the early land grants.

The architectural legacy of the first settlers remains almost unscathed in many places where the sandstone and early brick have sustained the temperate climate and pace of social change. Paraphernalia and memorabilia from the earlier colony are scattered across the state in shops and auction rooms as personal estates give up their history.

Tasmania encapsulates much more than the past that shaped it. The close proximity to Antarctica has made the capital, Hobart, a centre for scientific research while Launceston in the north is home to the Southern hemisphere's only Maritime College. Paradoxically, Tasmania has embraced the age of technology from the roots of her colonial past. Attracted by opportunity and inspired by the natural environment, a rich culture of literary, artistic and musical talent is embedded in the social fabric of urban and regional areas. Community life is valued highly and the strength of local communities sustains the network of towns and urban centres. The people are warm and friendly and happy to talk if you have the time and here on the island is the ideal place to take the time.

Ruins at Port Arthur from The Commandant's garden.

Evening light on The Hazards at Coles Bay, Freycinet National Park.

Open to the public, The Salmon Ponds, a trout hatchery and gardens, was established in 1861.

Hobart's Elizabeth Street Mall.

Plume Antiques at Campbell Town.

The Saturday market at Salamanca Place where the buildings date to the very early 1800's.

A peaceful evening on the Mersey River at Devonport.

Tulips in spring near Devonport.

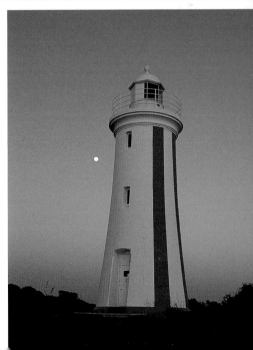

Far right: The Bluff lighthouse, Devonport.

City Centre, Burnie.

The tourist and fishing town of Strahan, centre for Gordon River wilderness tours.

Sleepy Bay, Freycinet National Park on Tasmania's East Coast.

Richmond Bridge.　　　*Button Bros. Store, Oatlands.*　　　*Red Bridge, Campbell Town.*

Prospect Villa circa 1830, Hamilton.　　*Worn steps at Oatlands.*　　*Woodcraft shop, Richmond.*

Moonrise over Launceston city from the Zig Zag track.

Moonrise over Cod Rock at Bicheno.

THE NORTH

Settled in 1806, Launceston in northern Tasmania is Australia's third oldest city. Nestled at the head of the Tamar River where the major tributaries of the North and South Esk River systems merge, Launceston holds all the charm of yesteryear while offering a contemporary, urban lifestyle. Reputed to have one of the largest collections of Georgian buildings in the world you need only to lift your eyes above the awnings of city shops to admire the historical streetscape originating from the early nineteenth century. Situated alongside the river, the city embraces the water front with fashionable restaurants, shops and accommodation. Boardwalks along the river's edge lead into the Cataract Gorge, a dramatic natural feature of water and rock that blends comfortably with Launceston's cosmopolitan lifestyle.

Beyond the city the grandeur of the wealthy settler homesteads defines the origins of early white settlement. Sandstone block and convict brick feature in many northern towns while the traditional low slung verandahs of English architecture typify the heritage of countless domestic buildings. Farming and tourism thrive amidst the legacy of colonial Tasmania. More recently, the increasing number of vineyards in the wine district of the Tamar river valley, although small mostly family run businesses, have earned international status for their exceptional, cool temperate wines. Many vineyards entice visitors with open cellars and boutique restaurants featuring the best of local produce.

The diverse geography of northern river valleys and dolerite mountains fall away to a sandy coastline dotted with holiday settlements of summer shacks and camping grounds, hollowed out of the Tea Tree scrub. The north westerly winds cool the hot summer afternoons, gusting across Bass Strait and the outer islands of King and Flinders. In winter the bluster whips across the beach in ever changing moods, sometimes soothing, often wild.

Launceston's Cataract Gorge in flood.

The Launceston City Park dates from 1806. The pear tree on the right, planted in 1827 could be the oldest frui[t] tree in the southern hemisphere. The Sebastapol Cannon, cast in 1840 in Russia and captured in the Crimea[n] War, was given to Launceston in 1860.

Boag's Brewery in William Street, Launceston.

The Colonial on Elizabeth, formerly Launceston Church Grammar School.

The Batman Fawkner Inn and Hotel Grand Chancellor.

Princes Square flanked by churches.

Bridestowe Lavender Farm at Nabowla.

Entally House at Hadspen, 1819

Farmland near Deloraine.

The old jetty at Bridport.

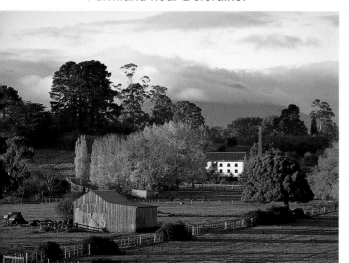

Vineyards and wineries line the banks of the Tamar River at Rosevears north of Launceston.

The National Rose Garden with over 2000 roses planted at Woolmer's Estate which was settled in 1816 by Thomas Archer.

The masculine dining room at Woolmer's replicating the lifestyle of the Archer family in the 1850's.

The chapel (1836) and bakery at historic Brickendon.

Launceston's Brisbane Street Mall.

Ben Lomond, one hour's drive from Launceston.

The Launceston suburb of Trevallyn reflected in the Tamar River with Richies Mill on the left.

The Pilot Station established in 1805 and the Low Head light house, mark the entrance to the Tamar River.

Winter dawn near Evandale beneath the Ben Lomond plateau.

Open to the public, Clarendon House near Evandale (left) and Franklin House at Young Town are owned by the National Trust.

Corner of Brisbane and George Sts.

Launceston Town Clock.

Cnr. Cameron and George Streets, Launceston.

Tamar Valley Resort, Grindelwald.

Queen Victoria Museum, Inveresk.

Country Club Resort, Launceston.

Historic Evandale.   Beaconsfield Gold Mine, site of a dramatic rescue of 2 miners in May 200

Sunrise on the Tamar River at Beauty Point.   Ross Bridge (1834).

The picturesque Liffey River in the Great Western Tiers.

THE SOUTH

Tasmania's earliest colonial history was written in southern Tasmania where Hobart (settled in 1804), has been the major centre of the state since 1812. Set on the River Derwent and in the lea of Mount Wellington, the unusual combination of mountain and beach makes Hobart unique, affording the benefits of opposing environments within a short distance of each other. The city retains much of its original architecture in public buildings, warehousing and private homes and combined with a modern lifestyle, presents a quality that is both exciting and inspirational.

Outside the capital, many smaller towns have also remained virtually unchanged in two hundred years. As the interior of the state was opened up beneath the relentless hand of European settlement, displacing the native population, the locally hewn sandstone provided an enduring material for the infrastructure of villages and pastoral homesteads.

Perhaps there is nowhere more renowned than the former convict settlement of Port Arthur where the harshness of the early penal system is difficult to dismiss as the weathered buildings testify to the purpose for which they were built. Ironically, the Tasman Peninsula on which the ruins of Port Arthur rest, is a landscape of striking beauty, with a sheer cliff line for most of its perimeter and deep, curved beaches to relieve the landscape of its drama. Walking tracks provide ready access to the spectacle of one of the most dramatic coast lines in Australia overlooking the Southern Ocean.

South of Hobart the Huon Valley, traditionally an apple and pear growing region, marks the entrance to the truly hidden wildness of some of Tasmania's priceless forests. Tall Eucalyptus and Myrtle trees with a thick moist undergrowth of rainforest flora provide a dense border around the mountains of the South West National Park. Explored by prospectors and adventurers in earlier years, today this corner of the island remains undeveloped and highly valued in an almost virgin state.

The Guard Tower on the banks of Mason's Cove at Port Arthur.

Nutgrove Beach, Sandy Bay beneath Mount Wellington in Hobart.

Wrest Point Casino, Hobart.   The May Queen.   The Shot Tower at Taroona.

Hobart city and the River Derwent from Rosny Hill lookout.

Mt. Wellington from Hampden Road in the historic suburb of Battery Point.

Lunch time break in Franklin Square.

Far right: Cascade Brewery (1824) is Australia's oldest brewery.

Hobart Town Clock.

Victoria Dock, the hub of Hobart's vibrant waterfront with Mures Seafood restaurant on the left and the Hobart Museum and Art Gallery in the centre.

Cruise boat, the Peppermint Bay on the River Derwent near New Norfolk.

Winter snow in the Mount Field National Park.

Early morning sun shines on the Penitentiary at Port Arthur.

The Church (1836).

Mason's Cove at Port Arthur.

Decaying convict built brickwork at Port Arthur.

The Penitentiary.   *The Guard Tower.*

Bullock driver, Brian Fish at Oatlands.

*Callington Mill at Oatlands
dates back to 1836 and is
now being restored to full
working condition.*

The Richmond Bridge, built by convicts in 1823, is Australia's oldest bridge.

View across Maingon Bay, the entrance to Port Arthur, to the rugged outcrop of Tasman Island and the light house.

Huon River dawn at Franklin.

A demonstration of the 'good old days' at Oatlands.

The peace and quiet of Bathurst Harbour in the vast South West National Park.

THE EAST

A scenic and popular spot for visitors, Maria Island to the north of the Tasman Peninsula lays a short ferry trip from the town of Triabunna. Also a former penal settlement, much of its history is still visible in the brick ruins of the convict stations. The island is home to the remarkable Painted Cliffs, a weathered rim of rusted limestone facing mainland Tasmania. Eastern Tasmania, like the interior, was given to free colonial settlers who were granted large tracts of lands for clearing and farming during the earlier part of the 19th century. Today, many local families are direct descendants of these earlier pioneers and still farm the same land. At the same time a thriving whaling industry took hold off the relatively sheltered coast line, where bays and inlets provided havens from the weather for smaller outfits to process their catch: boiling whale fat into oil before storing it in barrels for shipping to Hobart. Although lucrative, the industry lasted only approximately sixty years as whale numbers rapidly declined.

The milder climate of the east has seen clusters of traditional shacks and beach homes develop into seaside resorts, but while development has taken place, the coast retains an unspoiled shoreline. The panorama of smooth, pink granite peaks at Coles Bay on the Freycinet Peninsula is unrivalled in natural splendour. Better known for the spectacular views, walking and boating opportunities, historically, the area was territory for the Oyster Bay tribe of Tasmanian aboriginals. Further north, the seemingly endless stretch of beach along the perimeter of the Bay of Fires provides a wonderful opportunity to experience sun, space and relaxation away from any distractions.

Primary industry continues to sustain the smaller communities allowing long held family traditions of children following their parents into work. Timber harvesting and sawmilling, fishing and mining have prospered over the last two hundred years with the legacy of earlier technologies and practices now preserved in local museums and the collective, living memory.

Wineglass Bay and The Hazards in Freycinet National Park.

Boats set out on an early morning fishing trip from Coles Bay in the Freycinet National Park.

Surging waves at Sleepy Bay, Freycinet National Park.

The Painted Cliffs, Maria Island National Park.

Spiky Bridge (1834), near Swansea.

The Swansea Bark Mill.

Pegg's Point at Bicheno.

Far left: Bennett's Wallaby.

The Kangaroo Tail plant in flower.

Dawn at the Friendly Beaches, Freycinet National Park

Aerial view of the fishing and holiday town of Bicheno.

Sooty Terns and Silvergulls take flight at Diamond Island, Bicheno.

The Elephant Pass near St. Marys.   *Tasmanian Devils at East Coast Nature World, Bicheno*

Above: Denison Beach north of Bicheno.

Below: The road to the Blue Tier Reserve, Gould's Country.

The seaside town of Binnalong Bay near the Bay of Fires Coastal Reserve.

Silver Wattle blossom adorns the hills surrounding St. Columba Falls near Pyengana.

Above: Georges Bay at St. Helens.   *Below: Trousers Point, Strzelecki National Park, Flinders Island.*

THE WEST & NORTH WEST

The disparity in landscapes between the West Coast of Tasmania and the remainder of the island arises from the staggered line of mountain ranges dissecting the state which inhibit the rain laden winds from shedding on the flats beyond. As a consequence, the west relented more grudgingly to the tenacious efforts of the white settlers, yet by virtue of the almost impenetrable scrub, (and isolation from more amenable country), the earliest Europeans arrived at Macquarie Harbour and found it most suitable for a convict station. It became known as one of the harshest penal settlements in Van Diemen's Land, as Tasmania was then named.

The area around Strahan, in particular the Gordon River, produced a valuable resource in the Huon Pine tree, which permitted the development of an enduring ship and boat building industry, and provided a gruelling form of occupation for convict gangs in timber extraction. By the 1890's the abundance of minerals in the west was also being exploited with zinc, copper, tin, osmiridium and other mineral ores discovered. The small prospectors' claims flourished, became larger, commercial mining ventures and attracted larger populations. The towns of Queenstown, Zeehan and Rosebery today remain mining towns although much reduced in size since the boom days.

Toward the north coast, primary industry has invested in farming, where the volcanic red soils successfully sustain cropping and dairying. Historic properties such as Woolnorth in the far North West and Highfield at Stanley, maintain the legacy of the earliest pastoral company in Tasmania, the Van Diemen's Land Company, with their original homesteads and outbuildings.

Tasmania is one of the most mountainous islands in the world and the stunning rockscape of the Cradle Mountain – Lake St. Clair National Park in the heart of Tasmania is duly recognised and protected as World Heritage Area. The magnificence of the park with its repetition of lofty peaks and glassy tarns has seen this jewel of a landscape emerge as one of the premier icons of the state.

During clement weather, Cradle Mountain is a photographer's paradise.

Pencil Pine in the Cradle Mountain – Lake St. Clair National Park.

Weindorfer's Forest.

Flowering Hibbertia on the slopes of Cradle Mountain

World Champion axeman David Foster at Latrobe, where the Axeman's Hall of Fame and the Big Platypus attract many visitors each year. David is the holder of 183 world titles and the only person in sporting history to have won over 1000 championships.

The spectacular Meander Falls in the Meander Falls reserve, Great Western Tiers.

Winter at Weindorfer's Cottage at Cradle Mountain.

Pencil Pine Creek, Cradle Mountain – Lake St. Clair National Park.

Dillwynia glaberrina.

The Trapper's Hut at Lees Paddocks.

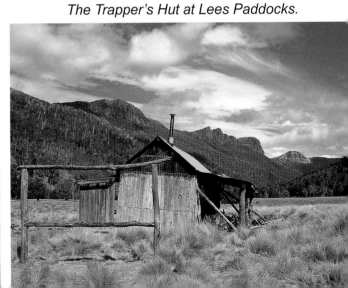

Marakoopa Cave in the Mole Creek Karst National Park.

The attractive beachside town of Boat Harbour.

A patchwork quilt of vegetables and poppies at Sassafras near Devonport.

Hay baling time near Sheffield beneath Mount Roland.

The rainforest of Eucalyptus and Myrtle in the Milkshakes Hills Reserve, 45 kilometres from Stanley.

The native Australian Echidna.

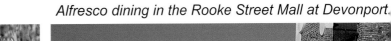

Alfresco dining in the Rooke Street Mall at Devonport.

Fields of spring poppies at Table Cape near Wynyard.

Historic Highfield House (1832).

Joe Lyon's Cottage, Stanley.

Spring time at the historic town of Stanley at the base of The Nut.

Clouds clear after overnight rain at Strahan.

The Lyell Highway winds its way to Queenstown.

A Wilderness Air flight lands on the Gordon River.

Dubbil Barril Station, West Coast Wilderness Railway.

Gordon River Cruise vessel, the Lady Jane Franklin.

World Heritage Cruise vessel, The Adventurer.

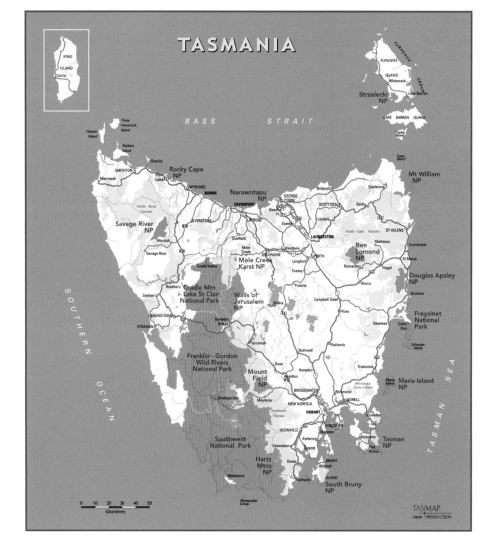

TASMANIA